D0515097

Teaching Listening

Ekaterina Nemtchinova

English
Language
Teacher
Development
Series

Thomas S. C. Farrell,
Series Editor

Typeset in Janson and Frutiger
by Capitol Communications, LLC, Crofton, Maryland USA
and printed by Gasch Printing, LLC, Odenton, Maryland USA

TESOL International Association
1925 Ballenger Avenue
Alexandria, Virginia 22314 USA
Tel 703-836-0774 • Fax 703-836-7864

Publishing Manager: Carol Edwards
Cover Design: Tomiko Breland
Copyeditor: Jean House

TESOL Book Publications Committee
John I. Liontas, Chair

Maureen S. Andrade	Joe McVeigh
Jennifer Lebedev	Gail Schafers
Robyn L. Brinks Lockwood	Lynn Zimmerman

Project overview: John I. Liontas and Robyn L. Brinks Lockwood
Reviewer: Soonyoung Hwang An

ISBN 9781942223030

Contents

About the Author

Ekaterina Nemtchinova is a professor of Russian and TESOL at Seattle Pacific University in the United States. Her publications focus on technology in language learning, teacher education, and the issues of nonnative-English-speaking professionals in TESOL. She is the author of *Listen Up!*, a Russian listening and speaking textbook.

Series Editor's Preface

The English Language Teacher Development (ELTD) Series consists of a set of short resource books for ESL/EFL teachers that are written in a jargon-free and accessible manner for all types of teachers of English (native and nonnative speakers of English, experienced and novice teachers). The ELTD series is designed to offer teachers a theory-to-practice approach to English language teaching, and each book offers a wide variety of practical teaching approaches and methods for the topic at hand. Each book also offers opportunities for reflections that allow teachers to interact with the materials presented. The books can be used in preservice settings or in-service courses and by individuals looking for ways to refresh their practice.

Ekaterina Nemtchinova's book *Teaching Listening* explores different approaches to teaching listening in second language classrooms. Presenting up-to-date research and theoretical issues associated with second language listening, Nemtchinova explains how these new findings inform everyday teaching and offers practical suggestions for classroom instruction. The book thus provides a comprehensive overview of the listening process and how to teach listening in an easy-to-follow guide that language teachers will find very practical for their own contexts. Topics include the nature of listening, listening skills and strategies, how to teach listening, using texts and tasks, and teaching listening with technology. *Teaching Listening* is a valuable addition to the literature in our profession.

I am very grateful to the authors who contributed to the ELTD Series for sharing their knowledge and expertise with other TESOL professionals because they have done so willingly and without any compensation to make these short books affordable to language teachers throughout the world. It was truly an honor for me to work with each of these authors as they selflessly gave up their valuable time for the advancement of TESOL.

Thomas S. C. Farrell

1

Introduction

Listening is a crucial part of daily communication in any language. It accounts for half of verbal activity and plays a vital role in educational, professional, social, and personal situations. It is also an extraordinarily complex activity that requires many different types of knowledge and processes that interact with each other. When asked which is more difficult in a foreign language, speaking or listening, many people would choose listening. Many teachers consider teaching listening challenging because it is not clear what specific skills are involved, what activities could lead to their improvement, and what constitutes comprehension. Students are also frustrated because there are no rules that one can memorize to become a good listener. The development of listening skills takes time and practice, yet listening has remained somewhat ignored both in the literature and in classroom teaching.

According to Nation and Newton (2009), it has been "the least understood and the most overlooked of the four skills (listening, speaking, reading, writing) until very recently" (p. 37). A current surge of scholarly interest in the nature of listening and existing approaches to classroom practice has brought about important new developments in the field. This book discusses up-to-date research and theoretical issues associated with second language listening, explains how these new findings inform everyday teaching, and offers practical suggestions for classroom instruction. Reflective Breaks scattered throughout invite you to pause, close the book, and consider these ideas in your own context as well as examine your approach to teaching listening.

2

What Do Teachers Know About Listening?

REFLECTIVE BREAK

• How would you define listening? Is it the same as hearing?

If your definition of listening refers to such concepts as interpretation, meaning, or comprehension, you have managed to capture its complex nature. When people listen, they interpret the incoming sounds and pick up important words from the flow of speech to construct meaning. They also make guesses about what they are going to hear next and check the new information against their predictions and knowledge of the world. Listeners use strategies to cope with difficulties of listening in real time. They try to remember at least part of what they heard and prepare an appropriate response in the case of face-to-face interaction. These processes are not separate; they happen simultaneously in the listener's mind and are interrelated with each other. This is why listening is described as an active skill: although their efforts are invisible, listeners have to work very hard to make sense of the aural input.

As a person hears a message, it enters the sensory memory, where it is stored in its original form for about a second. In this time, the brain distinguishes it from other noises, recognizes words of the language, groups them together, and either forwards the input to the short-term memory or deletes it depending on the quality, urgency, and source of the sound. The short-term memory keeps the input for a brief period to analyze it against the listener's existing body of knowledge. After the message has been understood by associating it with or differentiating it from the other information, it can be retained in the long-term memory forever. The brain, memory, and speech recognition processes are included in the cognitive dimension of listening (Vandergrift & Goh, 2009).

Equally important is the social dimension of listening, which accounts for its communicative nature. In face-to-face interaction, listeners are expected to show understanding by nodding, saying utterances such as *really* and *uh-huh*, making comments, and taking turns participating in the conversation. Even in a less reciprocal situation, such as a lecture, the listener could have an opportunity to respond, for example, by offering questions and observations. The social dimension of listening also includes gestures, body language, and other nonverbal signals, as well as pragmatic aspects of listening, which allow listeners to make inferences about the speaker's intention and determine implied meaning to respond in socially appropriate ways in a variety of situations (Vandergrift & Goh, 2009).

The cognitive and social processes of listening are generally similar in any language. Listeners who are nonnative English speakers (NNESs), however, face a number of additional hurdles in their efforts to understand aural speech.

REFLECTIVE BREAK

- Reflect on some of the ways that listening to a nonnative language could be difficult.

Listeners may miss part of or the entire message in their native language because they forgot what was said or could not hear very well. They also tend to tune out if a listening text is extremely long or uninteresting, or if they are distracted; however, their native knowledge of the language and culture helps them make sense of the input even if they failed to hear it in its entirety. Matters become more complicated when people listen to a foreign language, especially if they do not know it very well. Sounds blend together into a continuous stream; listeners get so caught up listening for individual words that they lose the thread of the conversation. Add to this situation the difficulty of different accents, colloquialisms, and fast-paced native speech, and listeners may quickly become confused. The short-lived nature of listening (as opposed to writing, where the words stay on paper) also increases the challenge: It is impossible to preview or review the message.

REFLECTIVE BREAK

- Does practice make perfect when teaching listening? Will students be able to understand more as they listen more?

The Process View of Listening

For a long time, listening instruction emphasized the importance of practice in achieving comprehension. Students were presented with text after text in the hope that extended exposure would improve listening comprehension with little or no analysis of how this comprehension was achieved. This method is called the *product approach* to listening. The emphasis on the product of instruction assumes that the listener receives the message and produces a single possible response to demonstrate her understanding (Field, 2008). It means that successful comprehension is determined by correct answers to questions and fill-in-the-blank exercises. The wrong answers indicate that the listener's comprehension failed at some point; the teacher would address the language and meaning mistakes but not the processes that lead to misunderstanding, so the student may well have the same difficulty in a similar listening situation.

To better understand the nature of listening comprehension, the *process view* of listening was adopted. It highlights the fact that, rather than simply taking the information in and getting the meaning out, listeners process input to create meaning from the incoming sounds and their own knowledge of the world. The process model treats listening as a complex interaction of cognitive, affective, and social variables to ensure reception, processing, and understanding of a spoken message (Vandergrift & Goh, 2012).

REFLECTIVE BREAK

- What are your views on the importance of product and process in the listening classroom?

Essential to successful comprehension is the listener's background knowledge and its influence on perception and memory. It is usually described in terms of the *schema theory*, which is based on the idea that all the knowledge that people carry in their minds is organized into interrelated patterns, or *schemata* (the plural of schema). A schema is a mental image of a particular situation or event, made up from previous encounters with similar events. There are two types of schema: *content*, which refers to general knowledge and life experience, as well as relevant knowledge of the subject matter, and *formal*, which reflects the listener's awareness of text types and genres. Cultural schema, which is also sometimes mentioned, describes familiarity with sociocultural norms of a given community.

In the process of listening, people invoke different types of schemata to render the meaning of the message. For example, when English native speakers from the United States hear the word *parade*, they think about people lining the streets to watch floats and marching bands. This is their schema for *parade*, which is very different from mine. I grew up in the Soviet Union, so my mental picture of a parade always involves military troops marching on Moscow's Red Square amid red flags. People all have their own personal schema shaped by their experiences; they understand new information by relating it to the existing schemata and predicting what they might hear next. The concept of schema highlights the importance of background knowledge in listening.

REFLECTIVE BREAK

- How can the knowledge of schema theory be helpful in teaching listening?

Bottom-Up and Top-Down Processing

When listeners listen, they make sense of the incoming information in two different ways. *Bottom-up processing* refers to deriving meaning from individual lexical, grammatical, and pronunciation items. It underlies the decoding process, from sounds to words and grammatical relations between them to sentences leading to overall comprehension. *Top-down processing* operates with existing schemata, ideas, and content. Rather than relying on discrete segments, people let their knowledge and expectations guide their understanding of what they hear. The two processes complement each other; the choice of one over the other depends on the topic, content, and type of the text. An example from my experience with audio books shows how top-down and bottom-up processes work together to ensure comprehension: I was enjoying Dan Brown's novel *The Da Vinci Code* and came across a phrase: "Langdon has hung NE PAS DERANGER signs on hotel room doors to catch the gist of the captain's orders." The bottom-up processing activated my minimal knowledge of French to understand the negation. The mention of hotel room doors invoked my general knowledge of hotels and made me think about *Do not disturb* signs before the next phrase, "Fache and Langdon were not to be disturbed under any circumstances," confirmed my guess.

REFLECTIVE BREAK

- Read the following text or choose a lecture from http://ocw .mit.edu/courses/audio-video-courses/. As you listen or read, take note of what you do to understand the content. Do you rely on top-down or bottom-up processing? When? What else do you do to get the meaning?

  Most spoken text differs in many ways from written text; therefore, the object of listening is different from that of reading. A comparison of a transcribed spoken text and a written text is likely to reveal a number of significant differences. Spoken text is fragmented (loosely structured) and involved (interactive with the listener). Written text, on the other hand, is integrated (densely structured) and detached (lacking in interaction with the listener). These functional distinctions are realized in certain linguistic features (Flowerdew & Miller, 2005, p. 48).

Listening to Comprehend or to Acquire the Language?

When teachers ask students to make predictions, discuss the main idea of the text, or summarize it, the primary concern is how well they understand what they hear. Teachers teach students strategies to facilitate comprehension and tell them not to cling to every word but to try to derive meaning from what they recognize. This approach encourages learners to rely on familiar language and provides little opportunity to boost linguistic development. It equates listening with listening comprehension, overlooking the important role listening plays in language acquisition. To help learners further their learning of the language, teachers can supplement comprehension goals, which focus on extracting information from the text, with acquisition goals, which draw their attention to linguistic features of the text, so that students explicitly notice them and incorporate them into their speech. This can be achieved by including activities that require "accurate recognition and recall of words, syntax and expressions that occurred in the input" such as "dictation, cloze exercises, and identifying differences between spoken and written text" (Richards, 2008, p. 87). Additionally, students could perform more productive activities requiring use of target forms from the text, such as reading transcripts aloud, sentence completion, dialogue practice, and role-playing. As learners work with transcripts and use the language in speaking activities, they master the forms they have heard. Extending listening instruction to develop students' abilities to understand oral speech and to acquire sound patterns, vocabulary, and grammar reflects the multifaceted nature of the listening process.

REFLECTIVE BREAK

- Reflect on a meaningful listening experience you have had. What made it meaningful or useful to you in terms of communication, new information, ideas, skills, language items, etc.? Alternatively, reflect on a lack of meaningful experiences and what may have been missing. How can this understanding inform your teaching of listening?

Listening Skills

A further insight into the nature of listening has been offered by the concept of skills. Skills can be described as automatic cognitive processes that ensure understanding of the language (Richard & Burns, 2012). As people listen, they assemble words from sounds, extract the meaning, and ignore irrelevant input without noticing these cognitive actions. An influential classification by Richards (1983) lists 33 conversational and 18 academic listening skills covering different levels of processing (e.g., sound, word, sentence, discourse). Here are some examples:

- discriminating between the distinctive sounds of the language
- recognizing stress patterns of words
- recognizing intonation patterns to signal information structure
- detecting key words
- guessing the meaning of words from context
- recognizing grammatical word classes
- recognizing cohesive devices
- inferring links and connections between events
- processing speech at different rates
- identifying the topic and following its development

Some researchers question the vague nature of a skill as well as the value of separating listening into smaller components, but others believe that a skills-based approach is helpful in analyzing weaknesses in the listening process. According to Field (2008), a skills-based approach provides a checklist that allows the teacher to pinpoint comprehension problems and give learners itemized feedback clearly indicating the areas that need more practice. Also, a skills-based approach sustains individual subskill practice in preparation for more comprehensive listening activities. To help learners make discrete abilities a part of their listening behavior, isolated skills training should be integrated with general comprehension work involving larger contexts and goals.

Listening Strategies

Another aspect of active listening is the variety of deliberate actions listeners take to achieve a particular purpose. When people listen to a lecture, they usually write down key words and concepts to retain information and review it later. Taking notes during listening is an example of a listening strategy. Those researchers who agree that strategies are critical in coping with listening tasks distinguish between *cognitive*, *metacognitive*, and *socio-affective* categories. Cognitive strategies, such as predicting and guessing words from context, help organize listening to complete a task, achieve comprehension, and promote learning. Metacognitive strategies, or thinking about listening, facilitate planning, monitoring, evaluating, and reflecting on the listening process. Asking oneself if the main idea is understood is an example of a metacognitive strategy. Socio-affective strategies involve communicating with teachers, classmates, and native speakers, as well as developing self-confidence and motivation. When students check answers in groups or seek additional practice opportunities, they use socio-affective strategies. Mendelsohn (1994), Flowderdew and Miller (2005), and Vandergrift and Goh (2012) provide useful inventories of listening strategies and describe how they can be taught in class.

Researchers continue to investigate strategies used by successful listeners and the effects of strategy training in nonnative language listening. There is a general agreement on the positive effect of such strategies, although some of them are more difficult to describe and teach than others. Rost (2011) names the following as effective listening strategies: predicting, inferencing, monitoring comprehension, asking for clarification and responding in an interactive exchange, and evaluating one's own listening processes. These strategies need to be discussed in class along with other actions successful listeners take to ensure comprehension. For strategy training to be effective, it should be incorporated into listening activities so that students can see how combining several strategies helps them gain in listening and self-confidence.

Reflective Break

- The theory outlined in this chapter describes the product and process views of listening, the interaction of bottom-up and top-down processing of aural information, the language comprehension and acquisition approach to teaching listening, and the concepts of listening skills and strategies. Discuss the implications of these issues for a group of learners you are familiar with.

3

How Can Teachers Teach Listening?

The research findings discussed in the previous chapter have several important implications for teachers. Although many aspects of the traditional listening classroom remain the same as in the past, the current view of listening as a many-sided interactive process necessitates a more comprehensive approach to teaching listening to help learners meet the challenge of real-life listening. Although listening is an individual activity hidden in one's brain, the teaching and learning of how to listen could be taken out of students' private domain into the public space of the classroom. The focus of instruction changes from whether comprehension is achieved to how it is achieved.

REFLECTIVE BREAK

- How was foreign language listening taught in your experience?

The Diagnostic Approach

Typically, teachers do some prelistening and then have students listen to the text and perform a variety of tasks. Teachers evaluate students' comprehension based on the correctness of their responses and proceed to the next activity. Implicit here is the focus on the result, the product of listening in the form of correct answers. This approach tests students' listening comprehension, informing them that they failed at certain points, but does little to teach how to listen, that is, to help them understand what went wrong with their listening and how it could be repaired. Field (2008) calls for a *diagnostic approach* to listening, which allows teachers and students to attend to listening difficulties and practice strategies to diminish them. Characteristics of the approach are described in the following sections.

Using Incorrect Answers to Detect Weaknesses, and Designing Activities to Help

How often do teachers rush to supply a "correct" answer when a student fails to respond to a listening task? Teachers may play a recording several times and ask for other students' input to make things right, missing an opportunity to determine the reason for the listening error. To revise this approach, a teacher could identify problems by making a note of students' lapses in comprehension as she checks their answers. She would then discuss with students how they arrived at a certain answer, what prevented them from understanding parts of the text, and what could be done to improve their listening facilities. Finally, she would follow up with activities that target specific listening problems that emerged during the discussion. The aim is to increase students' awareness of their listening processes and reinforce effective listening behaviors they can use when they face these problems again.

REFLECTIVE BREAK

- How can teachers best determine whether their students understand the listening material they give them?

Avoiding Listening Tasks That Require Memorization

Understanding a message does not mean remembering every single detail, so students' inability to recall information does not always signal a lack of comprehension. Yet some exercises—namely, multiple-choice and very specific questions—test listeners' memory skills rather than focusing on the listening process. Instructors should try to include various types of comprehension questions that discuss the content of the text as well as invite students to examine their listening performance.

Helping Students Develop a Wider Range of Listening Strategies

Ineffective listeners rely on a single strategy (e.g., focusing on individual sentences, missing the relationship between ideas) without changing or adapting it. To cope with difficult texts more effectively, students should be exposed to a variety of strategies. Explaining, modeling, and regularly practicing with students how to set goals, plan tasks, self-monitor, and evaluate helps them control their listening. Anticipating content, inferring, guessing, and recognizing redundancies improves specific listening problems. Encouraging interaction with classmates and native speakers through listening expands communicative contexts and enhances self-confidence.

Effective strategy use does not happen by itself. Although the very idea of strategies may seem to be too abstract to students, teachers can help them appreciate the importance of strategies by including activities with a focus on their listening process. For example, students could discuss (in small groups or with the class) what they did to prepare for listening, follow the text, identify key points, and so forth. Or the class could share personal experiences with various listening tasks and develop a master list of effective strategies for different types of texts, adding to it as their strategic competence grows. To introduce a strategy, the teacher needs to get students to realize that there is a problem and a way of dealing with it. She could model the strategy by explaining what she does and why it is helpful in this particular case, and provide multiple opportunities to practice in different listening situations. Depending on the task, she also could remind students to be flexible in their choice of strategies and to employ strategic listening outside of the class.

REFLECTIVE BREAK

- Make a list of listening strategies you are familiar with. Are there any strategies that seem more important than others? Why?

Differentiating Between Listening Skills

By identifying a set of distinctive behaviors that work together toward comprehension, teachers allow learners yet another glimpse into the listening process. Listeners may be used to employing microskills in their native language, but specific activities need to be designed to help them transfer those skills into a new language. Although each skill could be practiced separately, the key to skills instruction is not to treat them as a laundry list of discrete practice points that students get or do not get. Rather, skill training should become a part of a larger listening proficiency picture, inviting students to try new behaviors in a variety of contexts and tasks.

REFLECTIVE BREAK

- What is the difference between strategies and skills? How can this awareness help in listening instruction?

Providing Top-Down and Bottom-Up Listening Practice

The fact that listening is a complex multistep procedure that involves different types of processing implies that both *top-down* and *bottom-up* skills should be practiced in the classroom. Although many teachers tend to favor such top-down activities as comprehension questions, predicting, and listing, listening practice should incorporate bottom-up exercises for pronunciation, grammar, and vocabulary that allow learners to pay close attention to language as well.

Bottom-up processing helps students recognize lexical and pronunciation features to understand the text. Because of their direct focus on language forms at the word and sentence levels, bottom-up exercises are particularly beneficial for lower level students who need to expand their language repertoire. As they become more aware of linguistic features of the input, the speed and accuracy of perceiving and processing aural input will increase. To develop bottom-up processing, students could be asked to

- distinguish individual sounds, word boundaries, and stressed syllables
- identify thought groups

- listen for intonation patterns in utterances
- identify grammatical forms and functions
- recognize contractions and connected speech
- recognize linking words

Top-down processing relies on prior knowledge and experience to build the meaning of a listening text using the information provided by sounds and words. To arrive at a meaning of a text, the listener draws on her knowledge of the context, topic, speakers, situation, and the world, matching it to the aural input. Top-down listening skills include

- listening for gist, main ideas, topic, and setting of the text
- listening for specific information
- sequencing the information
- prediction
- guessing
- inferencing

REFLECTIVE BREAK

- Look at the list of bottom-up and top-down skills and think of specific assignments that target those skills. For example, to develop a skill of identifying thought groups, students can mark them in a transcript while listening.

Skilled listeners simultaneously engage in top-down and bottom-up processing, using both types of skills to construct meaning. Although pedagogically people often practice them separately because of their distinctly different focus, they can be addressed within the context of a single listening text.

For example, students are going to *listen to a 2-minute-long conversation about getting around the city. Before they begin, they are asked to *listen to sentences giving and asking for directions from the conversation and repeat them, paying attention to the intonation, meaning, and grammatical structure of each phrase. They do *a fill-in-the-blank exercise, choosing an appropriate form of the verb.

They *listen to a short monologue and trace the speaker's route on the map. They practice *asking and answering questions about different locations on the map. They have *a class discussion about getting to campus by using different kinds of transportation. Next, students listen to the conversation several times. They start by *listening to the first 15 seconds of the recording to make predictions about the topic and the setting of the conversation; they will *check their predictions after listening. Other while-listening tasks include *summarizing the conversation, *answering comprehension questions, *ordering the possible routes mentioned by the speakers, *listening for the bus numbers, and *a cloze exercise. After listening, students *discuss their predictions, *practice saying numbers, *act out situations asking for and giving directions, and *write a story based on a picture which clearly involves finding one's way in the city.

REFLECTIVE BREAK

- Categorize each of the starred activities above as either top-down or bottom-up. What is the objective of each?

The Role of Students

The process view of listening has changed the role of the listener from someone who was thought to passively receive the spoken message to an active participant in the act. Translated into the realities of classroom teaching it means that students take responsibility for their own learning how to listen. Instead of ingesting language and content, responding to comprehension questions when asked, and receiving instruction, they interact with the text and the task at many levels. They construct meaning by drawing on their schemata and switching between bottom-up and top-down processing. They employ a variety of strategies and skills, and discuss their effectiveness with their classmates. They rely on metacognitive abilities to overcome difficulties and seek additional opportunities to listen outside of class. By actively attending to their listening needs, learners improve performance in listening and learning the second language.

REFLECTIVE BREAK

- Vandergrift and Goh (2012) maintain that learners need to control their listening. What does such control involve? Why is it important? What activities would help students develop control over their listening process?

Another very important aspect of active listening is its social dimension. A typical listening textbook as well as most teacher-made material contains only recorded speech. Thus students cannot rely on facial expressions and body language to gain valuable cues to meaning, and they are missing the opportunity to communicate with the speaker as well. To approximate real-life listening experiences, students can be grouped or paired up to practice showing understanding or incomprehension, asking questions, agreeing or disagreeing with the speaker, and interrupting when appropriate.

REFLECTIVE BREAK

- As you read the following partial script of a lesson for low–intermediate students, think about the focus of listening instruction in this class. What is its main goal? What roles do the teacher and students play in this class? Consider the pros and cons of this approach. What would you do differently and why?

Teacher: We are going to watch a video about a Thanksgiving holiday celebration in the United States. What do you think people will be talking about at such a party? *(Students answer.)* Have you ever been to a U.S. Thanksgiving meal? *(Students answer.)* What is it like? *(Students answer.)* How about your country? Do you have something like that? A day of giving thanks? Is it different than in the United States? *(Students answer.)*

Teacher: OK, very good. Now, here are some words that we've learned. *(Points students to a vocabulary box on a worksheet)* You have to group them according to three categories. *(Gives students time to finish)* What do you have under beverages? *(Students answer.)* How about food? *(Students answer.)* What did you put into greetings? *(Students answer.)* What other U.S. traditions do you know of? *(Students answer.)* What could you add to each category? *(Students answer.)*

Teacher: Let's watch the video now. As you listen to the conversation, try to find answers to the questions on your handout. Let's read the questions together to make sure we understand them. *(Students read and discuss questions.)* OK, let's watch it.

After watching:

Teacher: What did you choose for the first question? Does everybody agree? What do you have, Fahd? What else do you have here? Oh . . . I think he said, *delicious.* Let's listen to this piece again. *(Students again watch the segment they did not understand.)* Did you hear that? *(Students nod.)* OK, question number two. *(Students answer.)* Right. How about number three? *(Students answer.)* Nobody got that? Let me go back there. *(Plays the segment again)* Did you get it? *(Students shake their heads.)* She says, *the last harvest.* OK. Number four. Why was he late? Tagrid, what's your answer? *(Student answers.)* Romina, what do you have? *(Student answers.)* Good job, everyone! We are going to watch it again. This time we'll focus on expressions they use at the table. Look at exercise number two on your handout. As you listen, circle the expressions they use. Did you find the exercise? *(Students nod.)* Any questions? *(Students say no.)* Are you ready?

After second viewing:

Teacher: So, what can you say to invite everybody to have a seat at the table? *(Students answer.)* What else can you say? *(Students answer.)* Pei-Chan? *(Student answers.)* Good! What does Shelly say to get the gravy? *(Students answer.)* How about drinks? How do you ask for a drink? *(Students answer.)* And if you don't want it? *(Students answer.)* All right. What did the hostess say to offer food? *(Students answer.)* Yes. And how did the guests thank her? *(Students answer.)* Very good! You got it!

Teacher: Now that you've learned the phrases, let's role-play. Imagine that there is a Thanksgiving dinner, and you are invited. Two students will be the hosts, the others will be the guests. Try to use the expressions we've learned. I'll put them on the board. *(Students work in groups.)*

The Role of the Teacher

REFLECTIVE BREAK

- What characteristics make a good teacher of second language listening skills?

When teachers teach, they seem to take charge of everything. They select input, design and sequence activities, determine tasks, and decide what constitutes a correct response. When several students give the desired answer, the teacher acknowledges their effort and moves on, never pausing to think if everyone in the class understood the text, and if not, what caused their confusion. When students make a mistake, teachers deem it their professional duty to immediately correct it. By doing that, teachers hope they are keeping the lesson going and also helping learners avoid the same mistake in the future. This approach puts the teacher in control of classroom activity and allows students to check the accuracy of their responses, but does it change students' listening behavior?

In a process-oriented classroom, the teacher assumes a more supportive role, facilitating rather than controlling and testing listening. She continues to manage the classroom business of planning, implementing, and assessing listening while taking a noninterventional stance in listening instruction (Field, 2008). Instead of presenting students with the correct answer, she guides them in comparing responses and reflecting on different steps they took to achieve comprehension. She encourages students to become aware of their listening, monitors their efforts, and provides feedback on their performance.

It is essential that students receive feedback immediately after the task, while they still remember the activity. At the same time, teachers do not want to embarrass weaker listeners in front of their classmates, so the discussion of common errors and ways to avoid them should be impersonal and nonjudgmental (*There were some problems with . . .* instead of *You made a mistake in . . .*). Personal feedback can be spoken or written; a quick in-class conference right after the activity may be followed by an email message with observations and suggestions after class. Individual comments should be transparent, targeting specific strengths and weaknesses and providing tips for improvement. A good strategy is to start with a general positive statement (*You did a great job understanding all the reasons the speaker stated*), mention areas for improvement (*I didn't see you taking notes while listening. Did you pay attention?*), and finish with encouragement (*You managed to understand a lot from the text*) to sustain confidence and create a positive listening environment where students are not afraid to try new strategies, make guesses, and discuss. To relieve anxiety associated with listening in a foreign language, I also tell my students about my own auditory problems (such as replaying phone messages eight times to get the phone number) and find ways to praise even their smallest successes to give them a sense of accomplishment.

REFLECTIVE BREAK

- What are your thoughts on the use of peer feedback in teaching second language listening in terms of its value, appropriateness, practicality, and guidance for students?

- Imagine that a friend is learning a new language and finds understanding oral speech particularly difficult. What suggestions could you give her to help her succeed?

4

Using Texts and Designing Tasks

In order to practice listening, students must have something to listen to. A variety of listening options is available both in and outside of class, so selecting appropriate materials requires some consideration.

REFLECTIVE BREAK

• What should teachers focus on as they choose listening texts for classroom work?

There is an endless variety of listening texts and situations; to classify them, consider

• the type of text (monologues or dialogues, spontaneous or prepared)

• the purpose (interpersonal—establishing and maintaining social relationships, e.g., small talk, greetings, or talking about sports—or transactional—providing and obtaining information, goods, and services, e.g., explanations, directions, or requests)

• the role of listener (participant or observer)

These variables can be combined in different ways to describe various instances of listening in real life.

Authentic and Scripted Texts

Many language textbooks are accompanied by an audio component. Usually, the listening texts are scripted, which means that the spoken discourse was first written out and then read and recorded. Scripted language is an effective teaching tool, but it lacks certain features of authentic input. The speakers speak rather slowly and seldom change the topic of the conversation. Their pronunciation is careful, intonation is exaggerated, sentences are complete, and there is no background noise to distract the listener. This is very different from authentic listening, which involves the language native speakers use in real life.

Educators have long been interested in the benefits and drawbacks of using authentic listening materials. On one hand, they allow students to explore the real language and culture and thus increase motivation and interest in learning. On the other hand, coping with the speed, vocabulary, and irregularities of native speech can make authentic listening very difficult, particularly for lower-level students. Moreover, because authentic materials are not accompanied by lesson plans and activities, they require a good deal of preparation on the part of the teacher.

Does this mean that teachers should stay away from authentic texts? The answer is *no* because both natural and scripted materials have a place and a purpose in a listening classroom. The choice of authentic rather than scripted listening is determined by the purpose of the lesson: Authentic texts are more suitable for learning to cope with features of native speech, and scripted texts promote working with specific language forms. It helps to think about authenticity as a relative rather than an absolute concept that could be modified to make authentic materials more accessible for listeners. For example, to control the level of complexity and manner of presentation, speakers could be given a topic and asked to improvise the conversation, which then can be recorded and edited for difficulties. They can also speak from notes, with natural pauses and repetitions, but using the vocabulary and structures within the students' grasp. The difficulty of listening tasks could be changed, too, to allow students to respond to an authentic text within their ability level (see *Planning Listening Instruction* for suggestions).

REFLECTIVE BREAK

- Could listening to a nonauthentic text be difficult? Why?

A scripted text can be demanding if it contains unfamiliar content, sophisticated vocabulary and longer sentences with embedded clauses, and requires complex cognitive processes to understand it fully. Lengthy (more than 3 minutes) texts with no visual support are tiring, too, because the listener's attention starts wandering after initial careful listening. To increase comprehensibility of difficult listening materials, teachers can do several prelistening exercises to activate content and vocabulary knowledge, assign listening to the same text multiple times with different purposes, and use a transcript before or after listening. Long segments can be presented in parts with comprehension-check activities between them.

Another consideration in selecting a good listening text is its relevance. Students will listen more carefully if the text is interesting and the vocabulary is practical. To increase students' involvement with texts, it is helpful to find out as much as possible about their backgrounds and interests and choose materials related to topics that will appeal to them. Another option is to list possible topics and sub-topics for students to choose from. Matching every single interest in class is unrealistic, but teachers should aim for the majority of students and hope that prelistening activities will arouse their curiosity.

In addition to authenticity, difficulty, and relevance, other important considerations in material selection are genre (e.g., narrative or description), register (formal or informal), and type of response (verbal or nonverbal). Ultimately, learners need to experience a variety of speakers, topics, purposes, genres, and styles to become effective listeners. Whether long or short, formal or informal, or featuring one or several speakers, listening texts should represent the types of spoken language that students can expect to hear in the real world.

REFLECTIVE BREAK

- Discuss the importance of such factors in material selection as authenticity, relevance, difficulty, variety, length, genre, and formality for your student population. Could some of them be more important than others?

Teacher Talk

A valuable source of listening (and one rarely recognized as such) is *teacher talk*. As teachers discuss classroom business, answer students' questions, or tell stories, they provide students with natural opportunities for interaction and practicing listening to unscripted speech. This type of input is the easiest to control for difficulty because the teacher can effortlessly paraphrase, repeat, explain, and change the speed of delivery. Keeping the benefits of teacher talk in mind, I try to resist the urge to address my students in their native language to save time when they ask a question about the target culture. I take advantage of their interest in the topic and make my response a listening activity. After announcing a purpose (*I am going to tell you about . . . After listening, you will tell me what you understood*), I tell the story at natural speed and then repeat it more slowly. I consciously monitor my choice of words and use of nonverbal cues, pause to check comprehension, and ask for a summary at the end.

Student Talk

Another natural source of aural input is *student talk* that emerges in the individual and group production during class work. Although some students and teachers object to cooperative activities because of the exposure to "poor" language and other speakers' mistakes, use of the native language, and perceived loss of control over the class, the advantages of collaborative work outweigh these concerns. Group activities provide an interactive and safe environment to practice aural and oral skills, maximize listening and speaking time, and enable even the quietest students to participate. Also, many learners find it easier to understand their fellow NNESs. When teachers notice groups of students slipping into their native language, they may remind them that every minute of the class time should be spent practicing the target language and that learning from each other is very effective because members of the group each have different strengths. To keep students on task, teachers should include relevant information-exchange communicative tasks with a clearly defined role for each participant and set a time limit for each activity. They should rotate group members to keep activities interesting and walk around the room while correcting oral mistakes, answering questions, and providing individualized feedback on listening and speaking. When students present individually, the rest of the class should be told to listen and ask questions, summarize, or report back.

REFLECTIVE BREAK

- In your experience as a second language teacher or learner, what were some activities that you considered helpful?

Listening Activities

Even the most engaging listening text is pedagogically useless if it is not accompanied by appropriate activities—a series of tasks that require students "to do something in response to what they hear that will demonstrate their understanding" (Ur, 1984, p. 25). Appropriate activities ultimately help students develop their listening skills.

Listening activities come in different forms and formats. They can focus on the main idea of the text or some specific information, require top-down or bottom-up processing skills, and ask for a verbal or a nonverbal response from listeners. The following classification of listening exercises is based on Rost's (2011) framework of different types of listening.

Intensive Listening

Intensive listening means paying close attention to the language of the listening text to single out words or phrases, grammatical structures, specific sounds, or intonation patterns. This accuracy-focused listening makes students consciously notice linguistic forms, which facilitates language acquisition. Although real-life listeners seldom listen in such a way, intensive listening activities provide valuable practice in perceiving the nuances of the language and should be included in a listening lesson. Some examples of intensive listening activities are

- transcription
- different types of dictations
- cloze (inserting words into blank spaces in a passage)
- dictogloss (listening to and then reconstructing a text)
- sentence completion
- error correction (comparing a spoken and a written text)

Selective Listening

Selective listening involves concentrating on specific details with a deliberate purpose in mind. It is usually done to extract information in response to a particular task, such as *Listen and say when the train leaves* or *Write down the telephone number*. Whereas intensive listening focuses on the precise language of the message, selective listening attends to essential bits of the content, disregarding irrelevant information. To engage in selective listening, students could practice

- following directions and instructions
- taking notes
- answering specific questions about amounts, dates, time, facts, and so forth

- predicting what will be said next after the recording has been stopped
- listing the sequence of steps, events, or topics mentioned in the text

Interactive Listening

Interactive listening requires the listener to participate in the conversation by alternating between listening and speaking. This back-and-forth interaction involves not only listening but also producing the language: negotiating the meaning, confirming understanding, taking turns, and delivering an appropriate response. It is the ultimate form of aural and oral practice that integrates linguistic forms, meaning, and social conventions of listening. Interactive listening practice can be done with peer students, teachers, or native speakers; because of the two-way nature of communication, these activities have a strong speaking component. Common interactive listening exercises include

- interviews
- discussions
- partial dialogues, in which students listen to a speaker and respond
- *information-gap* activities, in which students exchange information to fulfill the task
- jigsaw listening, in which groups of students listen to different parts of the message and then reconstruct the whole together

Extensive Listening

Extensive listening focuses on general comprehension of the text. It means getting the overall meaning and enjoying the content rather than seeking answers to specific questions. It exposes students to different voices and styles, improves automaticity in processing spoken language, and builds confidence in dealing with the spoken input. Extensive listening is appropriate for any proficiency level; however, because the texts are understood as a whole, they should not be exceedingly difficult. The following activities are based on extensive listening:

- summarizing
- rating content as more or less interesting

- using visual organizers (e.g., K-W-L [know, want, learn] and who/where/what/when charts)

- filling out listening logs, in which students record their listening goals and strategies for each text

- practicing flood listening, in which students listen to several recordings on self-selected topics

Responsive Listening

Responsive listening makes the listener relate to the content of the text by expressing an opinion, a feeling, or a point of view. Rather than appealing to facts, it elicits personal attitudes and emotions. This type of response may be colored by one's sociocultural background because the same content could cause different reactions from different cultures. Although responsive listening is more intellectually demanding because it requires both understanding and expressing one's reaction, its personal dimension appeals to many students. Examples of responsive activities are

- problem-solving tasks

- sharing and responding to personal experiences

- evaluative tasks, or making judgments about the truth, probability, and so forth

- paused listening, or responding to short parts of the text by making connections to personal experiences, world events, and so forth

- interpretative listening, or making inferences and deductions

Autonomous Listening

Autonomous listening describes any independent listening that is done outside the classroom. It promotes learner motivation and self-reliance because the choice of materials, comprehension monitoring, and task completion are determined by the listener. To help students cope with listening on their own, teachers can provide training in strategies and self-assessment techniques. Autonomous listening includes all the types of listening described in this "Listening Activities" section.

Reflective Break

- Here are some activities from a listening textbook. What type of listening is involved in each case? What activities could you add to make listening practice more complete?
  - — Choose verbs from a list that fit the logic of a situation.
  - — Guess the meanings of words and expressions from context.
  - — Tell what is going to happen next.
  - — Create dialogues after listening to either the question or the answer for the replica.
  - — Order events as presented in audio recordings.
  - — Listen to half of a dialogue and then recreate it in its entirety with a partner who has listened to the other half.
  - — Find intentional errors in texts.
  - — Make inferences about the speaker' intent.
- Think of a typical listening activity. What steps does it consist of?

Listening comprehension exercises are considered to be most effective when they are supplemented by prelistening and postlistening activities. Each of these stages has a specific purpose that contributes to building listening skills.

Prelistening Tasks

Prelistening activities are designed to set the stage for listening by activating students' vocabulary and background knowledge on a particular topic. In real-life listening people usually can guess with some degree of certainty what they are about to hear based on their knowledge of the situation, the topic, and the speaker. They also have a reason for listening, which determines how they are going to listen. Therefore, it would only be fair to prepare students for what they are going to hear in the classroom. The purposes of prelistening work are to improve comprehension, increase confidence, and arouse students' curiosity and motivation for further listening of the passage. Some examples of prelistening activities include

- providing the title of the text or playing the first few sentences to predict the content
- brainstorming key words or creating a semantic map associated with the topic of the text
- previewing vocabulary
- previewing comprehension questions
- reading and discussing a relevant text on the topic
- providing background information on the text
- discussing images related to the text or the topic

REFLECTIVE BREAK

- Think about all the instances of listening that occurred today. Did the way you listen change depending on the situation?

As you considered the preceding Reflective Break question, you probably noticed that in each instance today your attention to the listening material was different depending on the purpose of listening. As you listened to the traffic report on the radio on your way to work, you focused on your route and such words as *congested* and *bumper-to-bumper*, letting the rest of the report blend into the other background noise. When a colleague stopped you in the hall to chat, you continued thinking about your day, listening mainly to the tone of her voice and replying "Oh, really?" and "Wonderful!" when appropriate. When you attended a meeting on a topic that interested you, however, you paid attention to every word, took notes, and asked questions to clarify certain points.

When people listen in real life, they almost always know why they listen and what kind of information to expect, so they adjust their listening behavior depending on the purpose. When listening in class, students also need to know why they are listening to the text, what they need to focus on, and what response is expected of them. An essential aspect of prelistening is providing a purpose for listening. Having a purpose helps students listen more effectively, and yet teachers often forget to announce it. To enhance the success of the listening activity, clearly state the reason for listening and ensure that students understand the task before they hear the text.

Postlistening Activities

Postlistening activities serve as an extension of listening and make students apply the content of the listening text to a different context. These activities may be independent tasks that continue extending the topic of the text and help students remember the vocabulary, or they may be continuations of the pre- and while-listening activities. Postlistening activities allow learners to refine comprehension and learn more about the topic. As students engage in an active interaction with the language, teachers can use this stage of the lesson to integrate listening with other language skills, develop oral and written fluency, and evaluate the use of listening skills and strategies. After listening to a text, students could

- role-play and act out simulations
- create stories with different endings
- analyze the tone of the text and the emotions conveyed by the speaker(s)
- respond to the content of the text
- discuss the language of the text
- paraphrase or summarize the text
- discuss their use of strategies
- work on vocabulary from the text

REFLECTIVE BREAK

- What other pre- and post-listening activities could you add to the list?

Planning Listening Instruction

As you plan your listening lesson, think about the following:

First, does your activity match the type of text? Each listening situation requires a distinctive listening focus and specific tasks to support it. For example, the purpose for listening to a casual conversation could be to note topic shifts or the mood the speakers are in, whereas listening to a short lecture entails distinguishing main ideas and supporting details. Different texts lead to development of different skills, and teachers need to select listening purposes and activities accordingly.

Second, how challenging is this activity for your students? The overall level of listening difficulty could be modified throughout the task by changing the purpose for listening or the type of response required. Providing extensive previewing and visual support as well as shortening the text make listening more accessible too. Varying the speed of talk, the number of speakers, and the choice of more or less familiar topics and vocabulary are other ways of making a text easier.

Third, can you recycle your material? Most texts can be played several times with a different purpose for each listening (e.g., general understanding, specific information, and inferencing) to improve comprehension and build confidence.

Fourth, are you using a variety of tasks to target listening subskills? Include activities that focus on the word level, main idea, details, and prediction. Incorporate some extensive listening into your curriculum, and encourage students to listen outside of class.

Finally, even if the course you are teaching does not have listening as its main instructional goal, aural work could be integrated with speaking, reading, and writing so that different language skills reinforce one another. A listening text could serve as a context for grammar, vocabulary, and pronunciation practice or a warm-up for a reading activity; it could lead to a speaking or writing task in which students discuss a certain topic. By including a variety of skills in the lesson plan, teachers provide variety, balance, and an opportunity for students to develop a wide range of language abilities.

REFLECTIVE BREAK

- Think of a group of students you are familiar with who are NNESs. Listen to the text at http://www.esl-lab.com /tradition/traditionrd1.htm and imagine your students (a) listening to the text and (b) being interviewed in real life. What cognitive, linguistic, and social skills will they have to develop in order to understand the listening and participate in the real-life exchange successfully? Reflect on a sequence of classroom activities that can teach these skills.

5

Teaching Listening
With Technology

Language teachers have long used technology to practice listening.
From more traditional media such as analog audio and language labs
to newer, Internet-based media, technology helps provide learners with
authentic and realistic experiences that add excitement to the learning
process and increase their contact with the language.

Audio technology exposes students to a variety of speakers, voices,
accents, situations, and rich cultural content, and it affords additional
practice outside the classroom. It is easy to access and use at low or
no cost. Not only does it save a teacher's energy and voice, it offers a
listener a certain degree of control over listening. Whereas the real-
life voice is gone once the words have been spoken, a recording can
be paused and replayed as many times as needed to understand its
meaning. Audio technology can add interest to language instruction in
several ways. For example, a longer passage can be divided into man-
ageable portions by pausing at natural breaks. A teacher can also pause
listening to ask students to predict what they might hear next, write
an answer, transcribe a sentence, or simply repeat after the speaker for
pronunciation practice. Recording parts of an audio segment separately
can lead to an information-gap activity in which groups of students

each listen to a part of the text and try to reconstruct the whole story together.

An abundance of listening materials available in many different formats makes it easy to find an appropriate text for any student population. Some technology-based activities primarily focus on listening and others naturally combine listening and speaking, but most of them extend to practice of other language skills and strategies. They are easy to sequence and integrate into any curriculum, can be adjusted depending on the level of language proficiency, and work well in or out of class. Following are the most popular and widely accepted teachers' choices that can be used to teach listening comprehension in a variety of classroom settings:

- songs
- audio books
- radio (e.g., Voice of America, BBC, CNN, and Spotlight Radio)
- listening websites for ESOL (e.g., The English Listening Lounge, Randall's ESL Cyber Listening Lab, English Language Listening Online, Daily ESL, and Focus on English)
- video (e.g., commercials, documentaries, feature films, shows, and educational videos for native and nonnative speakers of English)
- podcasts (e.g., OhMyNews, ESL Podcast, and Breaking News English)
- academic lectures (e.g., ITunes University, Academic Earth, and MIT Open Courseware)

In addition to commercial listening materials provided by textbook publishers and digital audio on the Internet, many teachers prefer to make their own recordings to suit their teaching objectives and their students' listening needs. The following specific technology options do not provide content; rather, they are devices to present and deliver oral speech and teacher- and student-made recordings:

- audio and video recorders
- language labs
- Internet-based audio-recording platforms (e.g., Voxopop, VoiceThread, and PhotoStory)

- audio-recording and editing software (e.g., Audacity and Windows Movie Maker)

- online communication tools (e.g., Skype, Windows Messenger, and Google Video Chat)

- mobile phones and voicemail

REFLECTIVE BREAK

- Think of these examples and other types of technology that you have used or would like to use in the classroom. What are the benefits and shortcomings of each?

Actual classroom uses of these and other tools have been described in the literature (Flowerdew & Miller, 2005). If the technical details seem intimidating, search the Internet to discover a number of video tutorials on just about any tool, and play with the program or equipment to gain firsthand practice and become familiar with technology.

As you reflect on ways in which technology could supplement your listening class, consider the following:

First, whereas traditional equipment (e.g., audio and video players) may be primarily operated by a teacher, Internet-based technologies often require an active participation on the part of learners. It is important that teachers assess students' knowledge about computers before engaging them in an activity and provide training for those who are less familiar with technology. Students with no previous exposure to computers will need several training sessions to develop keyboard and mouse skills and learn some basic terminology. Provide a worksheet detailing the steps needed to accomplish an Internet-based activity to the entire class, even to experienced Internet users.

Second, always have a backup plan in case of technical difficulties. If using Internet-based materials, check the availability of the website immediately before the class. Recording the text on a CD or tape or reading it aloud from a printed transcript will save embarrassment and time if the Internet connection fails, the website is down, or the audio file does not open on the computer.

Third, it is a mistake to believe that playing a recording means teaching listening comprehension. Teachers must support an audio passage with a series of objectives; pre-, while-, and post-listening activities; and evaluation tasks, just as with any other activity. The same is true of cultural references embedded in the script. It is unreasonable to expect students to grasp a subtle cultural nuance on their own, so it must be brought to their attention, explained, and discussed. Finally, do not let technology make you lose sight of listening strategies, and include modeling and practicing those into your lesson plan as well.

Technology is an area of language teaching that changes very quickly. Some ways to keep up with recent developments and become familiar with new tools and their classroom applications are

- participating in professional workshops and conferences
- reading journal articles (e.g., *TESOL Journal*, *The Internet TESL Journal*, *Language Learning and Technology*, and *The Journal of Teaching English with Technology*)
- joining a professional online community such as a forum or a discussion group (e.g., NETEACH-L and TESLCA-L, two electronic mailing lists devoted to technology in English language teaching that are good places to start)

REFLECTIVE BREAK

- A student is interested in getting some additional listening practice outside of class. What suggestions and guidelines will you provide?

6

Conclusion

This book has attempted to summarize what is known about the nature and process of listening and relate theoretical issues to classroom instruction. Teaching and developing listening skills is challenging because the process of construction of meaning happens in the listener's mind and there is no direct access to it, yet the teaching and learning of how to listen effectively should be moved from students' private domain to the public space of the classroom for analysis and discussion. It is hoped that recent developments in research and practice have clarified such important issues as the focus on teaching rather than testing listening skills, the use of listening for comprehension as well as acquisition of language, the need for a multiplicity of strategies and skills, and the role of teacher and student in the process-oriented classroom, ultimately making teaching listening less challenging. Of course, each teaching situation is different, and what works in my classroom might not work in yours. Reflecting on how these ideas unfold in your classroom, reading books and articles listed in the References and Suggested Readings, and challenging yourself to try a couple of new things with your students will improve your understanding of how listening works and how you can help your students cope with it.

REFLECTIVE BREAK

- This book discussed the theoretical issues stemming from the complex nature of listening as well as practical matters, such as understanding various aspects of process-oriented teaching, choosing listening texts, designing tasks, and using technology to teach listening. Reflect on your practical approach to listening instruction in light of theoretical issues. What could you do to be a more effective teacher?

References

Field, J. (2008). *Listening in the language classroom*. New York, NY: Cambridge University Press.

Flowderdew, J., & Miller, L. (2005). *Second language listening: Theory and practice*. New York, NY: Cambridge University Press.

Mendelsohn, D. (1994). *Learning to listen: A strategy-based approach for the second-language learner*. San Diego, CA: Dominie Press.

Richards, J. (1983). Listening comprehension: Approach, design, procedure. *TESOL Quarterly*, 1, 219–239.

Richards, J. (2008). *Teaching listening and speaking: From theory to practice*. New York, NY: Cambridge University Press.

Rost, M. (2011). *Teaching and researching listening* (2nd ed). Harlow, England: Longman.

Ur, P. (1984). *Teaching listening comprehension*. New York, NY: Cambridge University Press.

Vandergrift, L., & Goh, C. (2009). Teaching and testing listening comprehension. In M. Long & C. Doughty (Eds.), *The handbook of language teaching*. Malden, MA: Wiley-Blackwell.

Vandergrift, L., & Goh, C. (2012). *Teaching and learning second language listening: Metacognition in action*. New York, NY: Routledge.

Suggested Readings

Anderson, A., & Lynch, T. (1988). *Listening*. Oxford, England: Oxford University Press.

Brown, S. (2011). *Listening myths: Applying second language research to classroom teaching*. Ann Arbor: University of Michigan Press.

Buck, G. (2001). *Assessing listening*. Cambridge, England: Cambridge University Press.

Campbell, C., & Smith, J. (2007). *English for academic study: Listening*. Reading, England: Garnet Education.

Davis, P., & Rinvolucri, M. (1988). *Dictation: New methods, new possibilities*. Cambridge, England: Cambridge University Press.

Flowderdew, J. (1994). *Academic listening: Research perspectives*. Cambridge, England: Cambridge University Press.

Helgesen, M., & Brown, S. (2007). *Practical English language teaching: Listening*. New York, NY: McGraw Hill.

Hinkel, E. (2006). Current perspectives on teaching the four skills. *TESOL Quarterly, 40*, 109–133.

Lynch, T. (2009). *Teaching second language listening*. New York, NY: Oxford University Press.

Lynch, T., & Mendelsohn, D. (2004). Listening. In N. Schmitt (Ed.), *An introduction to applied linguistics* (pp. 193–201). London, England: Arnold.

Mendelsohn, D., & Rubin, J. (1995). *A guide for the teaching of second language listening*. San Diego, CA: Dominie Press.

Nunan, D., & Miller, L. (1995). *New ways in teaching listening*. Alexandria, VA: TESOL.

Renandya, W., & Farrell, T. S. C. (2011). "Teacher, the tape is too fast": Extensive listening in ELT. *ELT Journal, 65*(1), 52–59.

Richards, J., & Burns, A. (2012). *Tips for teaching listening: A practical approach*. White Plains, NY: Pearson Education.

Rost, M. (2005). L2 listening. In E. Hinkel (Ed.), *Handbook of research on second language teaching and learning* (pp. 503–528). Mahwah, NJ: Lawrence Erlbaum.

Vandergrift, L. (2011). Second language listening: Presage, process, product, and pedagogy. In E. Hinkel (Ed.), *Handbook of research in second language teaching and learning* (Vol. 2, pp. 455–472). Hoboken, NJ: Routledge.

White, G. (1998). *Listening*. Oxford, England: Oxford University Press.

Wilson, J. J. (2008). *How to teach listening*. Harlow, England: Pearson Education.

Wolvin, A., & Coakley, C. (1992). *Listening*. Dubuque, IA: Wm. C. Brown Publishers.

Also Available in the English Language Teacher Development Series

Reflective Teaching (Thomas S. C. Farrell)

Teaching Listening (Ekaterina Nemtchinova)

Teaching Pronunciation (John Murphy)

Language Classroom Assessment (Liying Cheng)

Cooperative Learning and Teaching (George Jacobs & Harumi Kimura)

Classroom Research for Language Teachers (Tim Stewart)

Teaching Digital Literacies (Joel Bloch)

Teaching Reading (Richard Day)

Teaching Grammar (William Crawford)

Teaching Vocabulary (Michael Lessard-Clouston)

Teaching Writing (Zuzana Tomas, Ilka Kostka, & Jennifer A. Mott-Smith)

English Language Teachers as Administrators (Dan Tannacito)

Content-Based Instruction (Margo Dellicarpini & Orlando Alonso)

Teaching English as an International Language
(Ali Fuad Selvi & Bedrettin Yazan)

Teaching Speaking (Tasha Bleistein, Melissa K. Smith, & Marilyn Lewis)

 tesol
international
association

www.tesol.org/bookstore
tesolpubs@brightkey.net
Request a copy for review
Request a Distributor Policy